THE PAGODA

THE TOWER SKYLINE DRIVE

AN ILLUSTRATED HISTORY

by
CORRIE CRUPI

CHARLES J. ADAMS III
Editor

GEORGE M. MEISER IX
Historical Consultant

The Historical Society Press
of Berks County, Pennsylvania
1998

THE PAGODA • SKYLINE DRIVE

An Illustrated History of Reading's Mountaintop Landmarks

by Corrie Crupi

Charles J. Adams III, Editor
George M. Meiser IX, Historical Consultant

ISBN: 1-887762-05-1

Printed in the United States of America

READING'S PAGODA and SKYLINE DRIVE

INTRODUCTION

From "White Elephant" to the Symbol of a City!

by Charles J. Adams III

William Abbott Witman was a man of unusual vision.

While he was the renowned builder of residential and commercial buildings in the Reading area, he had flights of fancy which would lead him to erect such unconventional structures as the Circus Maximus, which, of course, recalled classic Roman splendor, and the Pagoda, his Asia-inspired triumph.

It was his dream to establish in the Pagoda a fine, unique hotel and restaurant.

It was his intent to place a massive bell on the top floor of the Pagoda and have that bell rung to mark the start of public events at the Circus Maximus.

Witman could not obtain the necessary licensing for his mountaintop hotel, and within a few years of its completion, the Pagoda Hotel concept was a shattered dream, and the Pagoda Bell was silenced.

The Circus Maximus, which survived for several years as a circus, sports, and fair grounds, was eventually enhanced with cement bleachers in the 1920s and now serves as Shirk Stadium at Albright College.

The Pagoda still stands high over the streets of Reading, a monument to Witman's vision.

Just a couple years after the courts turned down its builder's request for a hotel license, the Pagoda became what Reading newspapers called a "White Elephant" on Mount Penn.

Reading philanthropist and retired merchant Jonathan Mould gave the structure to the city in good faith, but officials in Reading were hard-pressed for ideas on exactly what to do with the novel building.

As the *Reading Eagle* covered city council's discussions as to what use could be made of the Pagoda, Reading residents responded with ideas of their own.

As the world learned of the Wright brothers' escapades at Kitty Hawk, one *Eagle* reader suggested, "Why not make it an aviation station?"

The newspaper added in cynical response, "Even the poorest kind of flying machine, in fact, one that has no wings, could fly from that elevation.

"All it would want would be a good start, and it would fly off into space. It would coast down into the city and might, with the accent on 'might,' make a safe landing."

The *Eagle* observation concluded, however, that the area would probably be unsuited as an aviation station. "Some aviator might bump into the Pagoda itself. It would not knock the Pagoda down. The aviator would have more than his feelings hurt, however, and the machine would be wrecked."

The newspaper presented other options. It could be turned into a "home for sickly children, or used as a tuberculosis sanitarium," or–something which proved to be a bit more practical–a place which would "sell light lunches, soft drinks, and other dry goods. Such a feature would make a big hit with the average Pagoda visitor."

Despite its sometimes checkered past, the many unfulfilled promises, unfinished plans, and unrealized dreams which have surrounded the Pagoda, generations of Berks Countians have grown up with the landmark tucked somewhere, somehow in their memories.

Whether it was an amorous night watching the lights of the city from a Skyline Drive lookout, a fun-filled day at a festival, a vigorous mountainside hike, or a heart-pumping bike ride, the Pagoda and the roads which lead to it are truly special.

Every year, high-powered sports car speed their way up Duryea Drive, and there was even a time when local college teams vied for the top prize in Bathtub Races from Penn's Common to the Pagoda.

The Pagoda's lights have served as signals for those in the valley below. Sports scores, the departure of Santa Claus from the North Pole, and other events were beamed below in codes coordinated by the newspapers and radio stations.

When Reading officially kicked off its 250th anniversary celebration on at the stroke of midnight, January 1, 1998, it did so by staging an unforgettable fireworks show from Skyline Drive.

READING'S PAGODA and SKYLINE DRIVE

Indeed, the scenic drives and verdant serenity of Mount Penn are irreplaceable resources, and the unmistakable profile of the Pagoda is the symbol of a city.

Master of the Mountain,
Guardian of the Vale.
Lighthouse of the Schuylkill,
Pagoda Proud, We Hail!

Symbol of a city
For Generations Past,
We Dedicate to Peace,
Eternal and Steadfast.

Charles J. Adams III

READING'S PAGODA and SKYLINE DRIVE

DURYEA and SKYLINE DRIVES

Formerly known as Mount Penn Boulevard, Duryea Drive was named to honor Charles Duryea, who is generally regarded as the inventor and builder of the first successful hill-climbing, gasoline-powered automobile in the United States.

The winding, climbing roadway was the perfect course for Duryea to test drive his invention from 1900 to 1907. Duryea also built his automobiles in his shop, which was first located at the foot of W. Elm Street on the west side of River Road, and later at 1712 N. 10th St. in northeast Reading.

When starting the journey onto Mount Penn by way of Duryea Drive, one will experience a road full of bends, curves, rises and falls until the summit of 1,200 feet above sea level is reached.

Road widths vary from 35 to 60 feet, and grades range from three to ten percent. In total, the road climbs about 2.5 miles and Skyline Drive stretches across three municipalities (Alsace and Lower Alsace Townships and the city of Reading) across the top of the mountain.

In the 1930s, the Pennsylvania State Works Progress Administration (PSWPA) workers made many improvements to the roadways on the mountain.

Among them was construction of a magnificent stone wall which still extends the length of Skyline Drive. Portions of wall also continue into McKnight's Gap at the northern end of the drive and onto the Pagoda plateau. The wall extends along List Road for approximately one mile, and curves onto Oak Lane on the northern down slope of the mountain. Along the drive, the wall breaks for three lookout points.

The erection of the wall was funded by the Federal government, under President Franklin D. Roosevelt. Workers were paid five cents an hour under the job program, which was aimed at providing work during the Great Depression.

In the Skyline Drive project, workers were given a receipt at the end of their work day, and were instructed to make the long trek down the mountain to City Hall, where they received cash for the voucher.

Construction of the roadwork on Skyline Drive commenced in February, 1932, and was completed on June 24, 1935 at a total cost of approximately $500,000.

As with most of the work of the W.P.A., the wall remains intact, as does a stone stairway at the base of the mountain. That stairway marks the start of a picturesque footpath which leads past an abandoned reservoir and a rock quarry.

The path climbs 295 steps from Penn's Common (Reading City Park) to the Rock Garden just below the Pagoda.

Little remains of the former Japanese Gardens and amphitheater which were once along the trail.

The "golden age" of improvements on the mountain came to an end with the start of World War II. By the end of the war, the Pagoda and Skyline Drive area had already fallen into disrepair.

Many factors, including natural erosion on the edge of the mountain ridge, led to a steady crumbling of many sections of the stone wall along the crest of Mount Penn in the latter part of the 20th century.

One of the missions of Pagoda-Skyline, Inc., has been to work with public and private sources to repair and restore the wall.

READING'S PAGODA and SKYLINE DRIVE

THE PAGODA

Easily the most famous and the most recognizable landmark in the city of Reading is The Pagoda, on the southern slope of Mount Penn.

The Pagoda serves as the curious identification of the city for many tourists and visitors. Its image has also been appropriated by many businesses and civic organizations, and most of all, it is the symbol of home for those who live in metropolitan Reading.

Few Berks Countians alive today can recall a Reading without a Pagoda.

The history of The Pagoda is clouded in legend, lore, myth, and hearsay.

The building was erected for William Abbott Witman Sr. by James and Charles Matz, contractors, between 1906 and 1908.

The intent was to erect a luxury hotel the likes of which no one had ever seen in Reading, or anywhere in the country.

READING'S PAGODA and SKYLINE DRIVE

It was the era of close-to-home mountaintop resorts. Mount Penn and its southern neighbor, Neversink Mountain, bristled with lively hotels in the early part of the 20th century.

But once completed, The Pagoda never became a hotel. Witman's application for a liquor license in 1910 was denied by a Berks County judge for several reasons.

The roads to The Pagoda were no wider than a cowpath, were unlit, and were deemed too hazardous for people who might have imbibed at the proposed hotel. The city refused to improve the roads, and the Pagoda Hotel was doomed before its doors ever opened.

William Abbott Witman Sr. and his brother had owned and operated a stone quarry on the site where The Pagoda now stands. Some say Witman wanted The Pagoda built there because he was embarrassed by the scar the quarry made on the mountain.

Remembered as "a feisty red-haired politician" and a *bon vivante* who had aspirations of becoming mayor of Reading, William A. Witman Sr. had alienated himself from many members of city council (then called "selectmen"). Witman served as a selectman, but never became mayor.

Why an "oriental pagoda" in the heart of Pennsylvania "Dutch Country?" For the novelty of it, of course.

There is slim documentation that Charles Matz, one of the brothers in the contracting firm which built The Pagoda, actually

suggested the final concept.

In 1942, the 84-year old widow of James Matz Sr., told the *Reading Times* that the building was based on a Philippine Island pattern.

Mrs. Matz said her late son, Charles, had served in the Philippines with the U.S. Army. "When he came home after the Spanish-American War," the newspaper reported, "he found that Witman was planning to build a tower on the mountain.

"Matz had seen pagodas in the Philippines, and drew a sketch of one for Witman, who adopted the plan and employed Matz's father as contractor."

That would dispel the notion that The Pagoda is of Japanese design.

It should be noted that a true *Japanese* pagoda of that era would never exceed five stories, would have not heat or running water, would be made of root trees, and would serve as a temple.

All this aside, The Pagoda was close enough to *looking* Japanese that during World War II, some Reading patriots demanded the building be destroyed

Mayor Menges was quick to respond, saying he was emphatically against razing the building. To further confuse matters, he justified his position by saying the structure was "Chinese," not Japanese!

The decades between the denial of the liquor license and World War II were tumultuous for The Pagoda.

Shortly after the court dashed Witman's dream of a mountaintop hotel, Farmers National Bank foreclosed on the property, and it was purchased by bank trustee and Reading businessman Jonathan

Mould.

Mould, who resided in a handsome home at 1246 Hill Road, was owner of the popular "Bee Hive" department store near 7th and Penn Sts.

On April 21, 1911, Jonathan and Julia Bell Mould presented The Pagoda and ten adjacent acres to the city for the token price of one dollar.

Mayor William Rick accepted the gift, proclaiming it to be an extension of "Penn's Common," Reading's city park which lies at the foot of the mountain and directly below the Pagoda.

In 1913, the city installed an electric pump to supply water to the Pagoda, and a year later the wooden railings on the balcony were reinforced with iron posts and wooden columns.

By 1935, the city had taken title to 1,595 acres of municipal land along the ridge of Mount Penn.

As the United States edged toward war with Japan in the early 1940s, something very curious happened in Reading.

Anti-Japanese sentiment was building, and several patriotic residents called for the demolition of Reading's "Japanese" Pagoda.

At some point during the controversy, the families of Charles and James Matz stepped forward with a post card picture which proved the Pagoda's Philippine design and soothed the paranoia of the patriots.

That post card is no longer in existence

The building weathered that wartime storm, and the Pagoda's hybrid heritage was affirmed.

READING'S PAGODA and SKYLINE DRIVE

The structure has had periods of rough-going as a ward of the city.

Just after the war, the Pagoda was closed to the public. It was restored starting in 1949 and eventually reopened.

On November 8, 1969, a short-circuit sparked a fire that damaged the roof and second floor landing of the east and west sides of the landmark. Assistant Fire Chief John Weinhold and Councilman Anthony Carabello commended the firefighters who fought the blaze against 12 miles-per-hour winds and prevented further damage.

That close call prompted city officials to install an automatic fire alarm system which had previously been voted down.

Reconstruction began on June 28, 1971 when 25 tons of scaffolding were wrapped around the entire exterior of the Pagoda.

The roof was replaced with 18,000 pieces of terra cotta tiles. The tiles weighed a total of 48 tons.

New lighting was provided by 850 40-watt incandescent light bulbs, 96 40-watt fluorescent tubes, and three miles of cables and wires.

Further reconstruction required 110 gallons of paint, 16 tons of new bolts, and 20 requested lions' heads.

The rededication ceremony was held December 11, 1971. So many citizens attended that Reading police had to enforce traffic and crowd control.

•

READING'S PAGODA and SKYLINE DRIVE

PAGODA TRIVIA

•The estimated cost to build the Pagoda was $50,000

•The building is 28 feet wide, 50 feet long, and 72 feet high

•The walls taper from five feet thick at the base to two feet at the top of the second story

•The first three floors of the building are made of stone from the adjacent quarry

•Each of the five overhanging, upswept corners of the building's roof recedes two feet from the one below

•The interior walls are made of concrete. The floors are plaster and trim is solid oak

•The Pagoda was, and is, dark red with yellow trim, and golden lion heads adorn the tip of each roof. A mythical pair of dragon dolphins crown the rooftop. They are said to protect the Pagoda from fire

•The Berks County Conservancy did its part in the restoration of the Pagoda by planting more than 10,000 trees on the site of the old quarry

•Inside the Pagoda are 16 small rooms and two large dining rooms. When first built, each room was furnished with a cot and a telephone for the convenience of guests

•The main floor is covered with red and yellow tiling, and there is a fireplace in the central room

•The original furniture included many Japanese rugs, dishes, lamps, vases, and other valuables. Much of it remains with the Witman family. Among the missing features is an original sundial and a "junrikisha," or cart which is said to have been the property of a Japanese emperor

•There are 87 steps leading to the observatory on the top level, from which a clear day affords a 60-mile view

•The lower level of the Pagoda is 886.91 feet above sea level. The top of the roof peak is 958.91 feet above sea level

FACTS FROM A 1945 CITY REPORT ON THE PAGODA

Observation and Fire Tower: Constructed in 1938
by the City of Reading and Public Works Administration
Cost of Structure: $30,493
Elevation Above Sea Level:
Door Sill (Ground Floor) 1,119.02 Top of Roof 1,239.02

MILEAGE DATA:

Duryea Drive, Penn's Common to Pagoda 2.25 miles
Skyline Blvd., Pagoda to McKnight's Gap 2.50 miles
Oak Lane, McKnight's Gap to Bern St. .75 mile
List Road, North Bend to Hill Road 1.50 miles
Angora Road, Egelman's Park to List Road 1.25 miles
Hill Road, Egelman's Park to List Road 1.25 miles
List Road to Antietam Lake .50 mile

READING'S PAGODA and SKYLINE DRIVE

READING EAGLE, SEPTEMBER 1, 1942:

WIDOW OF PAGODA BUILDER PROTESTS AGAINST RAZING IT

The widow of the man who built the Pagoda and the mother of the man who designed it yesterday asked Mayor Menges not to support any movement to raze the Pagoda.

The women's appeal was one of many that have been made to the mayor, who received two letters last week from a Reading man urging removal of the building which he described as "Japanese."

Mayor Menges, who was told in last week's letters that keeping the Pagoda on the mountain would "cost votes" if he seeks a second term, said emphatically that he is against razing the landmark. The mayor said the structure is Chinese, not Japanese.

Mrs. James Matz, Sr., 13th and Spruce Sts., 84-year old widow of the Reading contractor who built the Pagoda, told the mayor yesterday that the design is a Philippine Island pattern.

"There's nothing like it anywhere else in America," Mrs. Matz wrote, "and no other American city can boast of the gorgeous mountain scenery that can be seen from the Pagoda. It would be a shame to tear it down."

Mrs. Matz's son, the late Charles Matz, served in the Philippines with the U.S. Army. When he came home after the Spanish-American War, he found the late William A. Witman, city councilman for several terms, was planning to build a tower on the mountain.

Matz had seen pagodas in the Philippines and drew a sketch of one for Witman, who adopted the plan and employed Matz's father as contractor.

The Pagoda Bell

The bell which hangs inside the Pagoda was purchased in 1908 by William Witman as a decorative addition to his luxury resort.

At that time, the only Japanese couple known to reside in Reading were Mr. and Mrs. S. Miyanaga, who operated a Japanese merchandise store at 607 Penn Street. The Miyanagas aided Witman in his selection and purchase of the bell.

It was ordered through the A.A. Valentine Oriental import/export agency on Broadway, New York City.

Even at that time, anti-Japanese sentiment was building and the bell was shipped from Japan with tight security. It traveled via the Suez Canal to New York and by rail to Reading.

The bell was cast in Obata, Japan, in 1739 by a bell maker named Mikawaya. It hung in a Buddhist temple in Yakuozan until that temple was closed in the late 19th century.

Albright College political science student Akio Sashima began a two-year research project on the bell after visiting the Pagoda. Sashima's findings resulted in a renewed interest in the artifact.

On November 20, 1996, Japanese High Priest Tokujo Suzuki, of a Buddhist temple in which the bell was once housed, came to Reading and performed a ceremony which summoned spirits back into the Pagoda bell.

The bell was struck several times with a wooden mallet and Suzuki chanted prayers on behalf of the people of Reading and his home town, Hanno.

Suzuki was ecstatic about the discovery of the bell in Reading, and Reading Mayor Paul Angstadt was equally thrilled to share in the cultural exchange.

Mayor Angstadt presented the wooden mallet which was used in the ceremony to members of Pagoda-Skyline, Inc., who accepted it as a keepsake. It is displayed on the fourth floor of the Pagoda.

The inscription on the bell was translated by Kosho Yamamoto, courtesy of the Tokyo Chamber of Commerce and Industry:

The gong sounds from high on the peak of Yakuozan.
Down into the valley the gong resounds low and deep.
With the moon on high it sounds clearly in the heavens.
With the flowers into the land of the dead it peeps.
It will recall the dreams of the 'six realms.'
All over the lands, all Buddha lands, all over the cosmos, this sound will leap.

It has been established that the Japanese characters on the bell are actually a poem which represents six paths–one of which guides the deceased to heaven.

"The sound of the bell," it is said, "leads them to the right path."

Legend has it that to ring the Pagoda bell is to ensure happiness.

THE GRAVITY RAILROAD

The time: The evening of August 9, 1881.

The place: Benner Humma's Hotel, 10th and Washington Streets, Reading.

The cast: A group of movers and shakers from Reading's political, cultural, real estate, and press sectors.

The mission: A discussion about the feasibility of utilizing the natural resources of Mount Penn for recreational purposes–to do what had been done in Mauch Chunk, Carbon County–to build a railroad on Reading's mountain.

Seeds of dreams planted in the discussion amongst those folks that night would not bear fruit for another eight years, but what grew from those talks would provide a unique escape for a generation of Reading residents.

There was, of course, no Pagoda atop the mountain at that time. But there were parks, resorts, wineries, stunning views and cool forest trails–and even, for a brief time, a zoo–on or around the mountain. And, there were many people looking for things to do close to home.

Enter into the history of Reading the fabled "Mount Penn Gravity Railroad."

The "Gravity" provided the excitement of a mountain ascent through the beautiful glen overlooking the picnickers in Mineral Spring Park and onward to and through Egelman's Park.

Then, along a right-of-way which traversed the heart of the woods, the ascent continued across Skyline Drive to the "summit."

The steam locomotives pulled the old Brill-built open/closed cars at a speed which often topped 12 miles per hour. The 12-row passenger cars carried as many as 72 passengers each.

When organized in 1889, the Mount Penn Gravity Railroad Co. owned three locomotives–two 28-ton Shay gear types and a 22-ton Baldwin which could could tug two cars to the summit.

In the beginning, the cars were equipped only with hand brakes, but within a year, newfangled devices called air brakes were added.

The engines pulled the cars near the highest point of the 7.5 mile loop, but before reaching the summit the engines switched behind the cars and pushed the rest of the way.

At the summit, the engines retraced their journey and backed down the mountain to their starting point as the passenger cars coasted to the bottom of the hill.

The total trip lasted some 45 minutes, with cars operating at half-hour intervals. The fare was 20 cents per adult and 15 cents per child. Excursion rates were available, and discount passes (six for a dollar) were offered.

The tickets allowed riders to disembark at any of the stops along the way.

The landmarks along the tracks included Mineral Springs Park (and its hotel, now the East End Athletic Club), Egelman's Park, South Curve Gravity Park, Schwartz's Summit House, The Tower Hotel, Spuhler's Mountain Resort, The North Curve, Kuechler's Roost Winery, Reininger's Vineyard, Steigerwald's Winery, the School House Crossing at Spook Lane, Lauderbach's Spring, Miller's Family Park, Mt. Olympus Family Circle, Mountain Spring Assn., and Eagles' Mount Home.

It is estimated that Spuhler's Mountain Resort (later Haag's Mountain Manor) served 25,000 gallons of berry wine to more than 2,000 guests on an average weekend. That former resort was razed in 1977.

The presence of the railroad spawned much activity and interest in East Reading. Miller's Park Hotel (also known as the Pendora Hotel) stood at 19th St. and Cemetery Lane, and among its attractions were an outdoor beer garden, large ballroom, and picnic grounds. That structure fell in the 1930s.

And, at one time–for a short time–there was even a zoo in Pendora Park, which had grown to become a small amusement park. That facility was situated just below Sweeny's Dam, a popular swimming and fishing spot.

The first official ride on the "Gravity" was a major event, with company officials and invited guests filling the cars. The first women to ride were Sallie D. Missimer and Mrs. Charles D. Spohn, who happened to be on the depot deck in Mineral Spring Park on the occasion, and were asked to enjoy the experience.

The Gravity Railroad's corporate offices were at 536 Court Street in Reading, and the superintendent's headquarters was at the Mineral Spring Park station.

The stone and frame depot stood opposite the reservoir (now the tennis courts) under the present-day Lindbergh Viaduct. The ticket office was managed by G.T. Bassler. A railroad office was on the second floor.

The cement waiting platform was covered by an impressive wooden portico. A portion of the platform was still evident in Pendora Park at the time of the writing of this book.

Folks came from many miles around to ride the Mount Penn Gravity Railroad.

Several newspapers extolled the beauty of Mount Penn to readers throughout the state, with one account pronouncing: "The people of Reading are blessed in having such a charming retreat for the hot, sultry summer nights."

Indeed, 80,000 riders a year streamed onto the "Gravity" cars in its heyday, with that figure climbing much higher in a particularly good season.

But alas, the railroad rarely made a profit and never managed to pay off its debts.

In 1898, when the line was electrified, expenses were slashed but the railroad continued to lose money.

Prohibition in the 1920s added to the woes of local resorts, and the railroad suffered with them.

The death knell sounded for the "Gravity," however, when fire engine bells sounded in response to a devastating fire on April 26, 1923.

HORROR ON THE HAIRPIN TURN

Excerpt from "Great Train Wrecks of Eastern Pennsylvania"

by Charles J. Adams III

Its promoters touted a ride on the Gravity railroad to be "as if swaying in a balloon over the green billows below."

On Friday, August 22, 1890, that balloon broke.

The last major turn the passenger cars negotiated along their downhill glide before reaching the Pendora Park terminal was known as the "hairpin turn" by the nature of its tight design, and as "cemetery curve" because it overlooked Aulenbach's Cemetery in East Reading.

That Friday in August, that latter moniker was to become all too prophetic as tragedy struck the fledgling rail excursion line in its first full year of operation.

Charles Rettew had quit his job as conductor on the Wilmington and Northern Railroad to join the Gravity in a similar capacity. He was conductor for the morning runs that Friday.

In the 7:05 and 9:05 trips that day, all seemed well, except that one of the cars, No. 9, apparently hesitated when it reached Cemetery Curve during the 9:05 jaunt. The situation was not deemed critical, however, and the car was pressed into service again for the 10:05 trip.

Conductor Rettew manned his post, as did Frank Heller, the brakeman.

"The car had been inspected as all are before starting from the depot," Heller recalled. "When we had been pushed to the summit at the tower we tried to apply the brakes, but were unable to stop the car and it went down the gravity at an increasing speed."

Heller, who sustained internal injuries in the ensuing accident, was backed up by Cornelius Hanlon, a passenger on car No. 9.

Hanlon was a Reading Railroad engineer from suburban Philadelphia, and he and his wife decided to sample the Gravity Railroad ride on their way to visit friends in Pottsville. He had no idea what would happen that day.

"The accident was the worst I ever saw, although I have been railroading for a number of years," he said. "It is plain to everyone who knows anything about railroading that the engine left the car too quickly and that the car was running too fast. One of the chains broke and the other brakes were no good.

"I made a desperate attempt to stop the car when I saw the danger we were in, but when I found that the brakes were almost useless, I went into the car and told my wife of our peril. I wanted to take our children and jump, but my wife refused to leave the train.

"Believing that it was best to remain, we took seats on the floor in the rear of the car, holding the children. All the other passengers remained in their places, pale and trembling. The train must have been dashing down the road at the rate from 35 to 40 miles per hour!"

Other passengers concurred that the brakes had failed.

Howard Homan, another veteran railroader, said the problem was noticed as soon as the engine released the car at the Tower Hotel at the top of the mountain. He said the crew of the car made a valid and valiant attempt to slow down or stop the car.

As No. 9 rolled faster from the summit and it appeared that there were definite brake problems, brakeman Heller leaped from the car and ran ahead, hoping to purposely derail the car at a relatively flat area near Antietam Lake. The car beat him to the curve, and beyond that point was a winding, steadily dropping road which led to the infamous hairpin turn at the cemetery.

When Rettew saw that Heller had not made it to the curve at Antietam, he no doubt knew all was lost, and the runaway car was in the hands of fate.

As it descended along the straightaway which dropped on a 3.5 percent grade, the car rolled faster and faster.

Two women, one with a baby in her arms, jumped from the car as it sped toward the hairpin turn. They were determined not to chance what they felt would be much more serious injury if the car derailed on the tight curve. They all survived with minor injuries.

Witnesses said there were no screams of panic on the runaway car. Passengers clung tightly to anything they could. They cowered under seats, and remained stoic through it all. There was little they could do but pray, hang on, and hope for the best.

It was a quiet kind of terror.

Those last few yards and moments, as Cemetery Curve came into view and the sheerness of the cliff just beyond it was realized, must have been moments of sheer horror for those aboard car No. 9 that Friday morning.

Up to the very end, every able-bodied railroader on the car made fruitless attempts to apply the hand brakes. At about 10:30, all was lost.

The car swept into the curve and almost immediately twirled from the track and tumbled some 70 feet. Trees snapped and the earth was chopped as the fragile, open-sided car caved in, rolled, came to rest upside down, and hurled its passengers into a mass of writhing humanity.

When the wreckage finally settled, five people lay dead, and a score injured. Among the lifeless bodies pulled from the rubble was that of conductor Charles Rettew.

Rescue workers were at the scene almost immediately. What was left of the car was taken to the Gravity Railroad car barn on S. 19th Street, and the dead and injured were dispatched to morgues and hospitals.

Theories about the cause of the wreck and who was to blame were debated that day and well beyond. And while nobody wished to speak ill of the dead, many placed the blame directly on Charles Rettew, who had apparently made the decision to again use the same car which had some evidence of a problem on the earlier run.

One railroader who survived the wreck said the two types of brakes on the car interfered with one another, and the air brake mechanism prevented the hand brake from working properly.

Company officials said they doubted that was the

cause, but promised to investigate.

Car inspectors were quick to defend their actions prior to sending car No. 9 back up the hill after it had balked on the 9:05 run.

Joseph Monasmith said he rode both earlier runs, and had personally tested the hand brakes. They had been working fine.

Tyson Hafer acknowledged that Rettew complained that the hand brake stuck on the 9:05, but after he looked into it, he pronounced both braking systems to be in fine working order.

The railroad suspended operations the rest of that day, but as a coroner's jury was seated, the Gravity went back into service. On Saturday and Sunday, more than 2,700 passengers paid their quarters and dimes and took the ride. Some certainly came for the sweeping view from the top or the fresh, lush fields and forests of the slopes of Mount Penn. Others probably came for the morbid thrill of gazing upon the scarred embankment at Cemetery Curve.

After the wreck, certain additional safety precautions were taken, and only the hand brakes were used until mechanical investigations were completed.

The Coroner's Jury came to a fairly swift decision on the cause of and blame for the accident. The verdict stopped short of mentioning names, but was nonetheless to the point:

The fact that the 9:05 train stuck at the cemetery curve admonished all concerned that there was danger with the brakes. To put the blame on the conductor, or he with the brakeman, on the 10:05 a.m. train might be reasonable, but they should not bear the responsibility in acting as the agents for the company, which, it has admitted, employed brakemen and car inspectors who knew nothing about the brake lately adopted and which had not stood the test of experience.

The Mount Penn Gravity Railroad executives and employees had learned their lessons after the fatal wreck on Cemetery Curve that August.

Or had they?

On the afternoon of November 5, 1891, cars No. 1 and 10 careened off the tracks at another turn just south and west of Cemetery Curve. Two crewmen were killed, and the line immediately shut down for the rest of the season while safety factors were once again assessed.

That second accident resulted in sweeping changes to the right-of-way of the railroad. Runaway sidings and switchbacks were built to arrest any cars which would be speeding unabated toward dangerous curves. After those modifications were made, there was never again a serious accident on the Gravity.

Reading, Pa. View of Mt. Penn. Gravity R.R.

MT. PENN TOWER, READING, PA.

THE RISE AND FALL OF "THE TOWER"

Convinced that the Mount Penn Gravity Railroad needed a "marquee" attraction at the top of the mountain as an attraction, the railroad company in 1890 commissioned a magnificent stone dance and entertainment pavilion known as The Tower.

With a 40-mile view in every direction from its lofty position some 1,200 feet above sea level, the tower hotel became that sought-for destination for excursionists.

Thousands traveled to the hotel to enjoy the bowling alleys, pool and billiard parlors, shooting gallery, shuffleboards, refreshment stands, novelty booths–and even an amusement ride called "The Caterpillar."

Ice cream and soft drinks were sold at a booth located next to the tower, and flashing signs which read "For Men Only" beckoned males to plunk a penny in and have a peek at "Lingerie Ladies" or "The Three Peaches."

The Tower quickly became everything the "Gravity" promoters hoped it would be.

Its glazed dance floor could accommodate a thousand dancers, and was large enough even to allow couples to dance the "horse trot." That step had been banned on smaller floors because folks would too often collide at high speeds!

Pop bands played favorites such as "Beautiful Ohio," "Alexander's Ragtime Band," "The Trail of the Lonesome Pine," and other early "hits."

Eventually, such musical aggregations as the Germania Band, the Ringgold Band, the Reading Symphony Orchestra, and a house band called the Tower Orchestra were added to the mountaintop musical menu, and during the summer months there was music every day of the week in the hotel.

As the popularity of the Summit House and the Gravity Railroad increased, many people believed Reading could well take its place as a premiere resort city of the east coast.

The carbon arc and yellow gas lamps of the Tower danced in the sky at night (those lights could reportedly be seen as far away as Myerstown, some 21 miles away), and couples of all ages gathered in the romantic setting.

Young men would escort their dates for a bite to eat and a dance or two. The beaus

would be nattily-attired with suits, ties, and hats. The ladies would likely wear long skirts or gowns, high-buttoned boots with pump heels, white kid gloves, and large hats adorned with flowers.

A stroll to the top-floor observatory might have been in order, or perhaps a daytime visit to nearby Wildwood Park.

That park, just to the east of the Tower at Hill and List Roads, provided a cool retreat with fresh spring water and well-maintained picnic grounds.

While the Tower boosted the ridership of the Gravity and the reputation of Mount Penn, something that happened to it just before 7 p.m. on April 23, 1923 led to the demise of the railroad and the decline of Mount Penn as a resort area.

THE FIRE OF 1923

Monday, April 23, 1923. 6:45 in the evening.

Residents of the city look toward Mount Penn in horror.

The Tower is ablaze!

The fire quickly spreads from the north end of he dance hall to adjoining buildings.

From a signal light atop the Pagoda, the call is made for firefighters to ascend the mountain.

Frantically, the volunteers scurry. Even troops of Boy Scouts lend their aid.

There is little hope, however. With no adequate source of water on the mountain, firefighters from the Keystone and Washington fire stations are relegated to using chemical applications.

In short order, and despite all valiant attempts to douse the flames, the Tower is a total ruin.

As the embers cool, the investigation proceeds.

John Crum, a foreman of the Gravity Railroad, reveals to authorities that at about 2:30 that afternoon he noticed a suspicious individual loitering around the hotel. The man asked Crum to see the building, but Crum refused to allow him entrance.

Crum further states that around 5 p.m., he saw that same person hurrying from the direction of the tower.

As Crum tells his story, detectives sifting through the rubble make a sickening discovery. A bottle, half-filled with kerosene, and a box of matches are discovered at the scene.

The testimony and the evidence leads authorities to one conclusion. The Tower Hotel fell at the hands of an arsonist.

It is later revealed that there were threats to Henry Schwartz down at the Summit Hotel, and others had seen the strange man lurking about the hotel properties.

The day after the fire, some 1,000 people line up to ride the "Gravity" to survey the damage of the mountaintop hotel. A newspaper report notes that the sentiment of the people was so high that "if the arsonist had been caught by them, he would have been lynched."

All is lost. The Tower–its bowling alleys, its dance hall, and its position as a central attraction along the Mount Penn Gravity Railroad–will never rise again.

Many memories, some which were recorded in initials and graffiti carved into the woodwork of the Tower staircases, are up in smoke.

Local businessmen and government leaders make futile attempts to revive interest in rebuilding the hotel.

But people are finding other diversions. The automobile is giving them mobility. The mountain railroad is becoming a relic. No one seems to care anymore. Prohibition, and then arson, has doomed the "Gravity."

March 8, 1924: A railroad terminal, car barns, six electric motor trolley cars, five passenger cars, three trucks, tools, wire, and rails are purchased by George D. Horst for the paltry sum of $12,650.

Nature begins its consumption of the old rail rights-of-way. The ravaged Tower becomes an eyesore.

An ever so brief era has come to an ignoble end.

SCHWARTZ' SUMMIT HOTEL

After the fire of 1923, Schwartz's Summit Hotel, which had been built by William and Henry Schwartz in 1891 just a few hundred feet south of the Tower, became popularly known as the "Tower Hotel."

A well-built, four-story structure with 18 spacious bedrooms and 16-feet wide verandahs, the Summit Hotel was finely appointed. Its bar was supplied with fine liquors, and its wine cellar was well-stocked.

Private promenades for guests, the latest conveniences, and rocking chairs on the wrap-around porches gave the Summit a reputation for elegance.

What's more, a promotional piece for the hotel boasted, "The atmosphere is cool, dry, exhilarating, and free of malaria. There are no flies or mosquitoes."

But, with no rail and limited automobile access, the

Summit Hotel faced hard times in the late 1920s.

In 1931, the city took over the hotel, and after an unremarkable two decades as a public recreational facility, the building was slated for demolition in 1951.

Mayor James Bamford stepped in to give the old hotel a stay of execution, however, when in 1952 he worked out a lease with Eastern Radio Corporation, which would use the building as broadcast studios.

It was there that Reading's first television broadcasts were made over WHUM-TV, channel 61.

Only five years into a ten-year lease, WHUM asked, and the city agreed to break the agreement.

The time and elements-ravaged building finally met the wrecking ball in 1959.

Upon its solid foundation a picnic pavilion was built. But that, too, fell to neglect and vandalism.

At the time of the publication of this book, only portions of walls of the old Summit Hotel–which generations simply and erroneously called the "Tower Hotel"–remain as a reminder of Reading's once-prosperous and promising mountainside resorts.

THE WILLIAM PENN MEMORIAL FIRE TOWER

by Charles J. Adams III

As this book went to press, the tower atop Mount Penn stood as a monument to neglect and architectural abasement.

Of the tangible remnants of the glory that might have been Mount Penn, it looms as the highest point on the hill overlooking the city, yet it is a soulless corpse of a building, ravaged by disconcern.

And yet, it stands also as a pillar of hope.

The top of the stone structure peaks higher above sea level than the Empire State Building. The tower's neighbor on the southern slope of the mountain, the Pagoda, has become a symbol of the city while the tower is its orphan.

Actually located in Lower Alsace Township, the tower is a ward of city. But, it has become merely a stone post for elaborate communication devices and is devoid of any identity unto its own.

A generation or two have grown up in its shadow not knowing a thing about it. They know it as "The Tower," and have no idea how it ever came to be.

Indeed, the tower needn't have been so doomed to anonymity.

Born as a "make-work" project, perhaps the most tangible appelative ever given the building was the ignominious "Project PA-2136F" of the P.W.A. in the mid-1930s.

Yet, as we delve into the planning for the tower through the eyes of its architect, G. Cleveland Freeman of Mount Penn borough, we find that the project was perhaps more to its architectural father than simply a way to channel $15,091 in Federal Emergency Administration of Public Works grant money into the pre-war, economically-depressed city.

To be sure, the tower was commissioned to serve primarily as a Fire Tower.

In 1939, Reading councilman Howard McDonough reported that the city's 5,000 wooded acres could easily be viewed from the tower's vantage point, and with binoculars, puffs of smoke as distant as Valley Forge and the Delaware Water Gap could be discerned.

But as important as this utilitarian function was the tower's service as a recreational facility for an as-yet-unmobile Reading populace.

A generation that bemoaned the fire at the old Tower Hotel would be able to trek the 120 steel steps to heights hitherto unreachable.

The observation deck was open from early in the morning to late at night and the view was far superior to that from the Pagoda.

Thus, the tower enjoyed precious few years as a genuine rival to its more exotic neighbor.

We refer to a letter in the September 21, 1939 *Reading Times* from writer Lilly March:

> I can tell you that what you can see from the new tower is more than worth climbing all those steps for.
>
> All in all, it's pretty magnificent, and another plume in the cap of our fair city, about which I love nothing so much as the whole of Mount Penn, and what has been done to it.
>
> If you haven't been there yet, pick a good clear day and make for it quick as a wink.
>
> When the leaves have started turning it ought to be simply breath-taking.

State of the art illumination made the tower the beacon of Berks County. A glass-walled room contained 16 spotlights that sent 2,400 watts of light over the darkened landscape.

Another light provide red and white signals for communication codes.

It is interesting to note, however, that no matter what the building is today, it is not and never has been a mere tower of stone.

For G.C. Freeman, it was always much more–and had some of the ideas well-researched and conceived ever come to fruition, the tower may have served another function.

Let us start at the beginning, however, and save that "other function" as a surprise for those who were not privy to Freeman's unpublished and unapproved plans.

There are many components included in the design of Reading's tower.

Freeman searched via mail for those components, writing to owners of existing towers of stone from which to glean architectural bases for design.

Cosmetic and functional elements from more than a half-dozen towers were considered as the architect received photographs and post cards depicting them.

Some of those towers included a 75-foot fire tower in the Garrett Mountain Reservation in Paterson, N.J.; a water tower in Highland Park, St. Paul, Minn.; the Perkins Memorial Tower on Bear Mountain, N.Y.; the Clark County State Forest Fire Tower near Henryville, Indiana; Bowman's Tower near New Hope, Pa.; and the Pilgrim Memorial Monument in Provincetown, Massachusetts.

Some of those suggested specimens were provided by L.H. Weir, director of the National Recreation Association, to whom Freeman wrote for aid.

In addition to those architectural considerations, Freeman also proceeded with technical aspects of the more practical sides of the tower's *raison d'etre.*

The Supervisor of Aviation Inspection for the Pennsylvania Bureau of Aeronautics, Maj. R.G. Herbine, wrote to assure Freeman that since the proposed tower was not within 1,000 feet of an airport or along a duly authorized civil airway, no aviation warning light was necessary.

Still, Freeman included in his plans a 750-watt lighting fixture atop the tower. To provide an even more dramatic lighting capability, Freeman envisioned the use of glass blocks for a true "lighthouse" effect.

But the aforementioned "surprise" element Freeman incorporated in the "working designs" of the tower is the most remarkable of all his wonderful works.

The first hint of the mystery element came in a volley of letters sent to various suppliers on August 20, 1938 from the Carsonia Avenue office of architect Freeman:

"Writer who is designing a revolving type stainless steel roof, approximately 12-feet in diameter, to be used over an observatory, was interested in materials and fabrication."

An observatory?

True, the idea died on the vine, so to speak, but it is historically interesting to note that, yes, the man who designed the Tower Atop Mount Penn did at one time consider submitting a proposal which did include an astronomical observatory perched a hundred feet atop the stone shank.

Freeman's inquiries brought a sheaf of replies back to his office.

M.H. Schmid, manager of sales for Republic Steel Corp., suggested such roof fabrication be done by the C.E. Halback Co., of Brooklyn–designers and builders of the Chrysler Tower in Manhattan.

The Budd Company of Philadelphia showed an interest and offered to prepare an estimate of costs.

Other firms provided leads and ideas for construction of a movable observatory dome, and expressed their desires to be competitive should any design actually include the facility.

Freeman delved further into the possibility of an observatory, asking Bausch & Lomb Optical of Rochester, N.Y., to recommend a telescope which may be erected inside the dome. A hard-sell letter from L. Fischer of the company's Specialty Sales Dept., is interesting:

We want to remind you that you are perfectly free to purchase the popular B & L Prismatic or Draw Tube Spotting Telescope for a week's trial.

Try one of these fine instruments under different light and weather conditions–compare it with any similar scope you can get–and if you are not thoroughly convinced that the B & L Telescope is the finest you have ever seen or used, simply return it to us, for a refund of your money.

Isn't it true that cheap or mediocre equipment doesn't last a lifetime or give a really pleasing performance?

Our slogan, "The World's Best By Any Test" is no idle boast, although it is fully descriptive.

These "Prismatic" and "Draw Tube" telescopes had proven successful in collegiate observatories, and Fischer stopped short of apologizing for the $55 selling price:

It is no exaggeration to say that each model would cost well over $100 if it were not regularly produced in such tremendous quantities.

Despite the temptation of adding this dimension to the tower's intent as a fire observation post, and despite Mr. Fischer's selling prowess, the observatory was obviously not included in the final design of the tower as submitted to Reading city council.

After the P.W.A. approved its $15,091 grant on

September 15, 1938, and the city added its $18,445, the wheels were set into motion for the final design and subsequent construction of the tower.

The Freeman proposal was submitted November 8, 1938; the state Art Commission approved the design a week later.

The final approval of the project came from the Federal Emergency Administration of Public Works on December 5 and the consent to begin construction was given December 9.

Councilman McDonough, director of parks, wanted assurances that construction would take no more than 120 days. Thus, in the dead of winter, on a high, windy mountain, construction commenced.

It is interesting to note some of the specifications mandated in the P.W.A. regulations: "Preference in employment shall be given to persons from the public relief rolls," stated the preamble to the specs, which also included wage scales supplied by the Building Trades Council.

Bricklayers and stone masons were the highest-paid workers at $1.37 an hour. Plumbers received $1.20/hour; electricians, $1.00/hour; apprentice engineers, 95 cents/hour; and laborers, 60 cents per hour.

The government kept strict watch on the regulations it established.

On February 6, 1939, Williams Giles, resident engineering inspector, wrote to Freeman that Frank Sully and Phillip Boyer, two 60-cents-an-hour laborers, worked nine hours a day on two occasion, "constituting a violation of payroll regulations which I (Giles) shall be compelled to carry as a non-compliance."

The project was completed in August, 1939.

The tower did not open officially until October 28, 1939. As it rose proudly at the highest point of the mountain, a contest was held to give it a name.

A young man named Tony Pietrovito had watched the 1939 graduation class of Reading High School put on a program, "Penn's Dream." It came to him–The William Penn Memorial Fire Tower.

Pietrovito, a lieutenant in the "Boys' Nautical Club," submitted that name, and it was ultimately chosen as the official name of the new tower.

The dedication ceremonies for the tower were forced inside due to high winds on the mountain.

So, 150 citizens gathered in the ballroom of the old Summit Hotel to listen to brief speeches by Mayor Stump, Councilman McDonough, and Mr. Pietrovito.

The Reading Federal Band provided musical entertainment.

When not pressed into service during dry spells and forest fire seasons, the William Penn Memorial Tower played host to visitors from near and far.

In the first two months following its opening, an estimated 80,000 people visited the tower, and observers claimed automobiles bearing license plates from every state in the union came to call.

Unfortunately, the tower's "golden years" were few. Minimal maintenance and a diminished need for its fire observation services resulted in a steady deterioration of its interior.

It was used by the Division of Forestry until September, 1988, when the tower was vacated and its decline was accelerated.

The late William Richter, past chairman of Pagoda-Skyline, Inc., said of the tower in the mid

1990s, "I call it my wounded sentinel guarding the city. The Fire Tower has left an indelible mark on the landscape of Berks County, but it makes me ill when I see it now."

As this book went to press, Pagoda-Skyline, Inc., a group of volunteers dedicated to the preservation and restoration of the Pagoda, Skyline Drive, and the William Penn Memorial Fire Tower, was generating interest and funds to restore the tower, and had submitted an application for a federal grant to restore the landmark.

THE SKYLINE TODAY

Mount Penn, which forms a wooded backdrop to Reading, is more than ever a valuable asset and natural resource for the city and its metropolitan area.

Pagoda-Skyline, Inc., a non-profit group of volunteers whose mission is for the restoration and preservation of the Pagoda, Skyline Drive, the Fire Tower, and their surroundings, has taken the lead toward achieving those goals.

The newly refurbished Pagoda stands as a monument to the work of those volunteers and the generosity of the community.

Historical displays, art exhibits, and a Pagoda-Skyline,

Inc.-operated gift shop share space in the historic landmark with meeting rooms and, of course, the popular observation deck.

The Berks County Arts Council also maintains its headquarters in the Pagoda, which is open to the public six days a week.

Pagoda-Skyline, Inc. maintains a vigorous fund-raising schedule, with proceeds from its barbecues, "cruise nights" and other events plowed directly into restoration and preservation efforts.

Volunteers have organized trash-collecting programs utilizing crews ranging from scouts to prisoners in an ongoing campaign to keep ahead of thoughtless individuals who litter the precious mountaintop.

The guard railings at the lookouts along Skyline Drive have been replaced, and the Parks and Streets departments of the City of Reading have lent their support in the continuing improvements.

Immediate plans atop the mountain call for restoration of the William Penn Memorial Fire Tower and repair of the fragile walls along Skyline Drive. Erosion (and the occasional wayward automobile) have taken their toll on the 60+ year old stone walls.

Skyline Drive continues to play a vital role for many folks in and around Reading.

The winding road from Penn's Common to the Tower is the site of the annual Duryea Hill Climb, and the WEEU Cycle Series.

The circular plots which make up "Drenkel Field" are used by the "Flying Dutchmen," a group of remote-controlled airplane hobbyists, and various hiking groups trek the marked trails which crease the mountain.

And, hidden deeply in the wooded preserve of Mount Penn are the crumbling remains of the "golden age" of the railroads, resorts, wineries, and wonders on the mountain.

Grape vines once cultivated now wind wildly near remnants of old wine houses. Curious swaths of graded land cut through deep woods, marking the right-of-way of the old "Gravity."

The Pagoda, Skyline Drive, and the Tower continue to serve as an identification of the city of Reading, a symbol of home for all its residents, and a unique tourist attraction to travelers from around the world.

SKYlines...

Odds and Ends Related to the People and the Places of the Pagoda and Skyline Drive

•After the battle of Trenton on December 26, 1776, more than 1,000 Hessian soldiers were captured and sent under guard to Reading. They were held captive in small huts on the southeastern slope of Mount Penn, in a section of Reading still called "Hessian Camp." Terraces where food was planted by and for the prisoners are still in evidence on the sides of the deep ravine.

•Mount Penn was originally known as "Manor of Penn's Mount" when it was set aside as a preserve in 1748.

•Before the days of radio, news and weather conditions were flashed in code from a signal lantern atop the Pagoda. The code was broken by a key printed in newspapers.

•William Witman, builder of the Pagoda, also was the sponsor of the Pennsylvania State Baseball League. Witman conceived of the "Spring Street Subway," the underpass beneath the Reading Railroad Yards. Born in 1860, Witman was an unsuccessful candidate for mayor five times. He died in 1936, never realizing another of his dreams–a bridge across the Schuylkill River at the foot of Sixth Street.

•In 1939, blue lights flashed from the Pagoda to inform residents that the city had frozen the tennis courts in City Park and the ice was ready for skating.

•On April 7, 1942, the Pagoda lights were "blacked out" for fear of any enemy bombers which may find Reading.

•Easter Dawn Services were held at the Pagoda from 1914 to 1936. Originated by Rev. Franklin Cropp, pastor of First Baptist Church, the services were moved to the Tower when crowds got too big for the Pagoda grounds. The services are still held, and broadcast on Reading radio.

•At 9 p.m., Christmas Eve, the lights of the Pagoda are flashed off and on to signal children that Santa is on his way to Reading and it's time to go to bed. The tradition was started by Pagoda-Skyline, Inc., and is coordinated by the City of Reading's Electrical Department.

•An original Gravity Railroad bridge still stands, spanning the crest of Egelman's Dam along Hill Road.

READING'S PAGODA and SKYLINE DRIVE

ACKNOWLEDGEMENTS

PUBLICATIONS: *Historical Review of Berks County, Berks & Schuylkill Journal, Reading Eagle, Reading Times.*

BOOKS: *The Passing Scene*, Gloria and George M. Meiser, IX; *Great Train Wrecks of Eastern Pennsylvania*, Charles J. Adams III and David J. Seibold.

PUBLIC RECORDS: Berks County Recorder of Deeds, Office of the City Clerk, Journal of the Select and Common Council, Reading Historical Preservation Office, Reading Public Library Pennsylvania Room, Pagoda-Skyline, Inc. Archives, Historical Society of Berks County.

INDIVIDUALS: Jonathan "J.D." Del Collo, D.Michael Mucha, Akio Sashima, the Matz and Witman families.

•

This book is dedicated to the members of Pagoda-Skyline, Inc.–to their devotion and pride...and to the people of the City of Reading.
Special thanks to Pam McIntyre, Rita Richter, Laura Matz, and Marjorie and Carroll Keene.
And extra-special thanks to my son, Tony, who is most most avid listener and to my nieces Mandi and Steph Hoyer, who encouraged me to tell them stories of Skyline Drive.
And, I can't forget Mom and Dad Patton for the yard sale treasures and Ted, who walked beside me on the path back through time...
Also..."Dziekuje ci," Larry Soltys!

•

My hopes are to stimulate passion is this unique legacy of a once vibrant mountain top, the remnants of which are hidden throughout this mountain of ours.

Corrie Crupi

•

To a past filled with pride and a future filled with promise.

Charles J. Adams III

The Historical Society Press of Berks County, Pennsylvania
Reading, Pennsylvania
1998

Top: Construction of Skyline Drive, April, 1932. Bottom: Mt. Penn Gravity Railroad tracks wind past Schwartz's hotel. (Courtesy of the Historical Society of Berks County)

READING'S PAGODA and SKYLINE DRIVE

An undated photograph of "The Tower" (Courtesy of the Historical Society of Berks County)

Spuhler's Hotel (later Haag's Manor) was a popular stop along the Gravity Railroad line. This photo, by Wayne E. Homan, depicts the former hotel building as it appeared in 1964. (Courtesy of the Historical Society of Berks County)

Top: The refreshment stand at Schwartz's hotel is a busy place in this undated photo. Bottom: The Mineral Springs Hotel, a popular spot along the Mt. Penn Gravity Railroad line.
(Courtesy of the Historical Society of Berks County)

Top: A lazy day on the porch of the Tower, ca. 1920. Bottom: A nice day prompted many folks to picnic at the fire tower, as seen in this ca. 1950s photograph. (Courtesy of the Historical Society of Berks County)

A rare photograph of the bowling lanes at the Summit Hotel.
(Courtesy of Larry Soltys)

Top: A Mt. Penn Gravity Railroad tandem passes through open countryside on its way to the mountain. Bottom: Only the lower right wall of the former Summit Hotel remains as a reminder of this once magnificent mountaintop building. (Courtesy of Larry Soltys)

The Summit Hotel, as seen from the observation deck of the fire tower.
(Courtesy Charles J. Adams III)

READING'S PAGODA and SKYLINE DRIVE

Top: The entrance to Duryea Drive at City Park, just after the turn of the 20th century. Bottom: Skyline Drive and the Summit Hotel, ca. 1950. (Courtesy Charles J. Adams III)

Top: Kuechlers Roost, a legendary "watering hole" along the Gravity's route. (Courtesy Charles J. Adams III) Bottom: A rare photograph of the stone quarry which stood where the Pagoda now stands, ca. 1906. (Courtesy of Larry Soltys)

APPENDIX No. 9.

COMMUNICATION FROM THE MAYOR.

Submitting Letter from Jonathan Mould, Presenting to the City of Reading the Property Known as the "Pagoda."

To the Presidents and Members of the Select and Common Councils:

GENTLEMEN:

I am enclosing to you a letter which I received from Mr. Jonathan Mould, in which letter he presents, as a gift from his wife, Julia, and himself, the property on Mt. Penn known as the "Pagoda," together with ten acres, more or less, of mountain land. I also submit to you the deed which has been tendered to the city.

This is a magnificent gift, coming at an opportune time. The land presented forms a connecting link between the flag-pole and the boulevard, going a great way toward bringing all the land on the southwestern side of Mt. Penn, in that particular section, under the ownership of the city.

This gift is especially notable in, that it is given by people who were not born here, but who came to Reading and prospered with it, and have grown to love and be loved by the city and its people.

The Pagoda is the most prominent point in and around this locality, and can be used for various purposes for the benefit of the people in our nicely growing park system.

The generosity displayed by this gift is greatly to be admired and appreciated, and I am satisfied that your honorable bodies will pass the necessary legislation to accept the Pagoda and the land.

Respectfully submitted,

Reading, Pa., April 24, 1911. WILLIAM RICK, *Mayor.*

Honorable William Rick, Mayor,
City of Reading:

My Dear Mr. Rick:

Referring to our conversation of a few days ago, I herewith enclose deeds from Mrs. Mould and myself for the "Pagoda" property on Mount Penn, which we wish to present to the city as an extension to the present park and boulevard system, and for the enjoyment and benefit of the community.

We are very glad to be in a position to do this, as we have derived much pleasure ourselves from these mountains and have always advocated the idea that the city should own and control as much of this western slope as possible.

We hope this gift may be accepted and appreciated in the spirit in which it is given, and that it may prove a great pleasure and a real advantage to all.

Yours very truly,

Reading, Pa., April 21, 1911. Jonathan Mould.

A copy of the entry in the Reading City Council Journal, April 24, 1911, which paved the way for the donation of the Pagoda to the city.

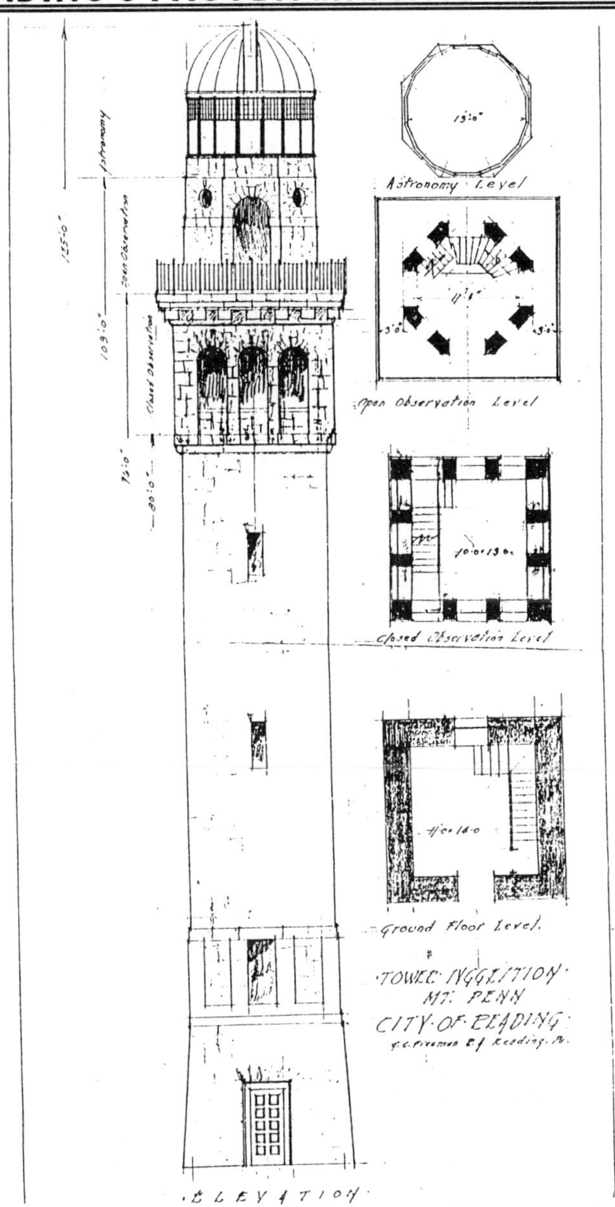

An early architectural rendering for the proposed fire tower on Mount Penn. Note the "astronomy level" which was planned.

Jonathan Mould, who donated the Pagoda to the city, was the proprietor of this department store in downtown Reading. (Courtesy Larry Soltys)

READING'S PAGODA and SKYLINE DRIVE

Top: A ticket stub for a ride on the "Gravity."
Bottom: Skyline Drive has been the symbol of the city in many ways, including a stylized version which appeared on this custom bank check.

William Abbott Witman, Sr., who commissioned the construction of the Pagoda atop Mount Penn.
(Courtesy of Mrs. Carroll W. Keene, great granddaughter of Mr. Witman)